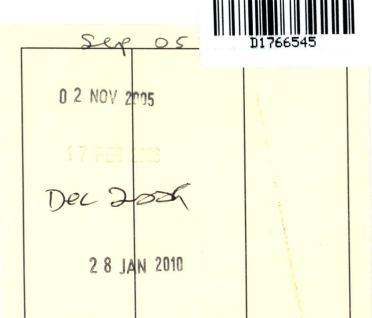 

SHOOK FOIL

KWAME DAWES

PEEPAL TREE

First published in Great Britain in 1997
Peepal Tree Press Ltd
17 King's Avenue
Leeds LS6 1QS

ISBN 1 900715 14 7

To Lorna, Sena, Kekeli and Akua

Oh, morning, at the brown brink eastward, springs —
Because the Holy Ghost over the bent
World broods with warm breast and with ah! bright wings.
G.M. Hopkins

So hit me with music
Brutalise me with music
Bob Marley

CONTENTS

SOME TENTATIVE DEFINITIONS I

"Lickle more drums..."
Bob Marley

First the snare crack,
a tight-head snare crack like steel,
rattle, then cut, snap,
crack sharp and ring at the tail;
calling in a mellow mood,
with the bass, a looping lanky
dread, sloping like a lean-to,
defying gravity and still limping
to a natural half-beat riddim,
on this rain-slick avenue.

Sounds come in waves
like giddy party types
bringing their own style and fashion,
their own stout and rum,
their own Irish Moss
to this ram jam session.

Everything get like water now
the way steady hands
curve round a sweat-smooth waistline,
guiding the rub, the dub, so ready.
This sound is Rock Steady
syrup slow melancholy,
the way the guitar tickling
a bedrock drum and bass,
shimmering light over miry clay.

LIGHT LIKE A FEATHER, HEAVY AS LEAD
Bob Marley, "Misty Morning"

All green light seeping into the morning
the smell of coconut oil and ackee,
lazy reggae pulsing through the thin boards.
This sleeping Sunday morning,
the hymns of the Pentecostal church
tucked into the dense green of August Town
swim like prophecy in waves
threading through the faint drum and bass
of the transistor chatting upstairs.

I hear Marley's thinning voice
cut after cut until I ache
from the apprentice cicatrices,
ears now alert to the gravel thin wail
of the original shortass reggae organizer
dubbing me bloody truths from the thin
concentric grooves – round and round
maddening gyre of prophecies,
spiraling mysteries and no clue,
no vision of some monumental journey
over strewn palm fronds and the praise of believers
through holy Kingston – the prophet slips by unnoticed;
(Jamaicans have never understood the hysteria
of Beatlemania, we die, not for pop icons,
but for sweet-mouthed politicians, we die).
This black, glowing vinyl of trapped sound
is all that is left, all that is left
of the rhygin, word-weaving prophet.

My fingers stretch and flow through
the whisper of old revelations like mist,
the rough of the cracked snare and one drop
sound is washed by something of a dream,
I cannot find my way through the smoke.
It is hours before a long-time-coming
sea breeze, still warm from its journeys,
tickles the morning; everything giggles,
everything is light as mute anomie,
while she closes his stiff eyes.

PISGAH

*"Til from Mount Pisgah's lofty heights,
I'll lift my wing and take my flight..."*

I did not know this then, since the sound
reminded me of life stirring at the bottom
of the sea, glinting fish, flaming coral
all flashes of energy coming like the lock-step
of a rhythm-section getting it right and tight;
gummy as beach heat and the smell of fish;
a mad man dancing to oblivion in Half Way Tree.
A way of making it all livable.
Since the sound was life-making,
I did not know it was a dirge,
a lamenting anthem to the Natty Dread's
unmoored spirit making its final journey:

passing down First Street
then skipping on to Second Street,
skanking through to Third Street,
wailing a prayer on Fourth Street,
lighting up souls on Fifth Street,
talking to two dread on Sixth Street
trying to reach, want to reach
gotta reach the Seventh Street
cause somewhere there is heaven street;
owning every crack in the concrete,
loving every scraggly stunted tree,
naming the dry ghetto beachhead,
a mystical place of cremated souls;
he dances the streets of Trenchtown
re-loving the path of survival, Natty Dread!

Then like wind he makes his last swooping pass,
sea winds fingering guitar strings,
then gone, then gone, then gone, then gone.

BLESSED ARE THEY WHOSE WAYS ARE BLAMELESS

A poet repents of his words

1

I make deals with the wind,
  blow the other way, I say,
blow the phalanx of spiraling black,
  the other way, I say,
and I will draw a new path of love,
  a new path of truth
for my treacherous soul. My lies,
  my dubious narratives
shall be cleansed with new light,
  and words spoken will unveil
the hidden wounds like carefully peeled
  gauze. My old lovers
will find their love in sheaves
  in dank places, and instructions
on what to do with them after wading
  through old streams of nostalgic
syrup: Burn them, burn them all!
  I have obeyed the precepts
of the one whose fingers have wiped
  salt tears from my eyes;
and so now I sit among the eternal horde
  contemplating the centuries
of purest impossible light with the saints
  and in truth I long to ask for
a brief reprieve from the holiness of this place,
  only for a while, just to breath again
the sensuous funk of a sweating dance hall.

These are the vulnerable mutterings
of a weak man, a man in search of the will
   to love the law like good food.
Today, I long to be called blessed,
   I long to face death without fear
of being discovered for the fake I am.
  So I write my lamentations
like psalms discarded by the harp-playing
   poet, who knew first love, a good line,
and the sound of God in the wind.
  I am stumbling now, as you can tell,
spoiling the deal with truth; but hold,
   I pray, the destruction of that
phalanx of twisting wind, or wrap me
   in a garment of courage, so when it lifts
me and carries me among the debris and dust
   to other landings, other gentle landings,
I may sing of your goodness and love
   and seek out the eyes of the saints
in the land of the living and the dead.

SOME TENTATIVE DEFINITIONS II
"Brutalize me with music..."

Into this sweet, well-made bed
slips the high tenor
of the lead man, dream man,
front man, don man,
face guy, lover guy,
with lyrics like water,
washing down, washing down,
fingers slow on the skin.

"Baby but yuh jus' won' let me"

He makes a poem of grunts,
the impromptu gutturals
framing the lyric's clean edge.

This is poetry walking a bass line,
this is poetry darting sweetly
around the rigid lick of the rhythm guitar.

Pungent like a wet mango,
the smell lingers in the skin
when the sound has passed.

CAUTION

The news comes like a stone:
cancer devoured his upful locks
and a sister collected the clumps
of carefully nurtured holiness
in a plastic bag to be matted
into a wig like a crown for the
bald Natty Dread in his casket.

He fell so low and the chemo seemed
like treachery. It all turned
worthless, this fighting, this
scramble for a cure, a way out;
this confession of mortality:

*Oh Jah, Oh Jah, why has thou
forsaken thy son? Oh Jah,*

*the veil is black like this night,
black like the treacherous road;*

*when it wet it slippery,
see me sliding, tumbling down;*

*see how this sickness make my soul
black as jet, caution, caution,*

*and my brothers, all they can say
is walk, walk, walk, walk, walk,*

*like the bubbling syncopations
of the synthesizer's left hand jumps.*

But who will walk with me,
who will carry the lamp on this path,
whose breathing will reassure me
of a company waiting on the other side?

My brethren will forsake me,
I walk into so many dark places
while I wait for the coming of light.

Reggae rides the air waves
and this island sound dark
for the passing of a song.

I AM A STRANGER ON EARTH

"I'm alone in the wilderness, I'm alone..."

Culture

1

There are days when this unfamiliar earth
   speaks to me and calls me
stranger, alien, brief sojourner here.
   It comes with the discovery of a new flower
the name of which I study with devotion and awe;
   or the way a sudden storm whips
the fallen leaves and bends the trees.
   I stand in the mind of the storm,
I feel like an obstruction – dispensable.
   The earth never tells me my true home.
I have never seen it, not even in dreams;
   I have no assurances that it is there.
I sit among stones and dried bramble
   and feed on the mysteries I can find
taking shape after the rain of tongues
   from the congregation gathered outdoors
to meet the light of sun, like white sheets
   put out to bleach on zinc in the blaze.
Here, I tighten my eyes to block out the dizzy
   distraction of spinning leaves,
of these strange flowers bursting about me.

2

Sometimes, when the head is giddy,
when the body finds its pulse,
   when the read word becomes an incantation
of light, like a rightly deciphered poem,
   I see faces of my enemies,
the arrogant and proud builders of snares,

wincing at the swoop of vengeance; a sword
falling, falling on them, upon them.
    Grown men weep and grovel for mercy
as the sword descends. I feel no remorse
    since this carnage is of another life
I do not know or understand. Besides, the wrath
    of the Almighty, so tutored
in the stench of bloated flesh,
    the quick expiration of last breaths
before his stony stare, is,
    as they say, his business,
and for us, all there is
    is trying. The spilling of blood
leaves me drained and tender
    like the soft place of a lanced boil.

3

    I stir from my trance hungry and thirsty,
and as sudden as a prayer formed, the sky is ashen-
    heavy, sputtering pellets of rain.
I stand before the language of this storm
    again an alien, a sojourner, waiting for a clue
to lead me homeward – a place of quiet rest.
    I know there is a truth in the storm,
but I do not delight in truth; I tremble
    for truth will shackle me
to this unfamiliar earth where guilt, regret,
    remorse for the blood drying in my nails,
must mark my waking moments. I have become comfortable
    as an alien at heart, free of the tyranny
of truth. In this rootless state my poems
    like prayers follow no prescribed path,
but record the slaughter of the wicked
    with cool remove. I embrace my fate
while the wind and water spin about my head.

SOME TENTATIVE DEFINITIONS III

"inna rub-a-dub style…"

Bob Marley, "Bad Card"

In this sound garden,
this constant ground swell
of music relentless as a pulse;
like an engine freshly fired;
or the sweating congo man,
thighs hugging the sides
of a smooth cylinder of sound,
beating, beating a pattern;
waiting on, waiting on,
waiting on the spirit to come,
so that with every repeat,
there is magic found,
a new way of seeing things;
in the monotony, a new way
of understanding sound.

This is the promise reggae
thrives on, the promise
that suddenly so, without rhyme,
without reason, the body
a go merge with the groan
of a circular bass-line, booming
and the rest will be the magic
of doing impossible things,
never the same again.

Without the fat bass
rumble, there can be no
blue of a harmonica coming
and going like uncertain breath;
no purple guitar slipping

20

like a hypodermic under the skin;
no Hammond drone and then trill
to stir up bumps on the skin.
This way, there is always something
to return to after the hanging
silence of a stripped-down version,
counting out the unspoken pulse,
then wheel and come again.

NATURAL

for Bob Marley

In the silence, the silence of
a new void of morning, I taste
the bitter weed of loss, like mauby,
like a forerunner to my own loss –
staring at the open autopsied corpse
of the body that housed my father,
lamenting only that which may have been,
lamenting that sometimes we die
before poetic justice can mete its magic:
Oh the things that could have been!
The dead young are impossible equations.
Morning, morning, I walk along the leaf-strewn
avenues of the campus, a sun-specked
day; the blessed light on my upturned face
making me think of the confession you made
at Cane River where on the rocks you laid your head,
there in desolate places to make your bed,
to make music; I find the stones here
take to the alchemy of poetry so well.
I walk like a poet in search of remembrances.
The slip of my memory gathers images
and tosses them among the turning leaves
to let fall something like rain
on a blazing hot day, rain-water touching
soft asphalt and making steam as sweet
and reassuring as incense in the sanctuary.

SILENT

1

The scrappy heads of ten year olds
  throw down gigs whose nails
chew into the flesh of the earth.
  In the dust storm, the children
are unmoved, they become one colour,
   they return to their origins.
I watch and imagine an eternity
  in this conceit: dust to dust.
I let the ash turn then settle in my mind.
  My purity is no longer intact –
it lasted for months; I lived
  in this pristine place of devotion,
where my mind was blocked to every
   wayward sound. The music of the city,
I blocked; the sound of voices, warm
  in the steamy nights, I blocked;
the pounding of my heart in dreams
  of laughing women, I blocked;
the trigger of anger and the orgasm
  of its flaming, I blocked;
till in this monk silence, I found power.

2

  Celibacy, I find, breeds a mind
as clear as Augustine's stark cubicle.
  It is true. My old sins come
on the wave of music. Debauchery is a sound.
  I find my mouth filled with red noises,
and then the fall is irrevocable.
  This is why I have run towards the vacuum
of silence, not to hear, but to not hear.

Watching the boys in their mute dance
cloaked in the turning dust, I understand epiphany,
   I understand the silence of piety.
Afterwards, the open lot is dotted
   by flowering pox with delicate
rims of the finest sand where the gigs have spun.
   Entering the void of their departure
is like entering a chapel of red hues.
   I study the silence, restored again, renewed

SOME TENTATIVE DEFINITIONS IV
"lick samba, lick samba…"

The girl them a shock out,
preening their garments,
imported from New York,
there on the edge of the crowd.
Everything round on them,
blossoms like bas-relief,
and when they breath,
a still water ripples
circles of undulation.
You will find nothing
to hold onto in their eyes,
transported as they are
by the bashment
sounds. They are waiting
like warm, panting, idle vehicles
before a red light
in sequins and pastels;
everything is riding
from batty to titties,
everything in place
but threatening
a chaos
of unleashed
body parts.
Green.

RUMOUR

"My brother, my brother,
my dearly beloved brother...
is dead..."

Culture

Who knew, who knew if the news
of his shedding locks in clumps,
his frailer body, his hollow eyes;
who knew, who knew if the news
of a dread gone to pot
was nothing but Babylon lies, lies
like the street telegraph would say,
like the sisters and brothers
labouring their salty way through
Kingston's dry rot would whisper:

Is murder Babylon a try murder the dread;
how a man must live so far from home,
far from yard, with all that stinking smell
of atomic energy and debauchery,
all that sodomy and crack like a curse?
Is murder Babylon a try murder the dread.

Who knew, who knew if the news
was lies to obscure another plot
dem a plot to kill another prophet;
and being so far away, across a phlegmatic,
unfeeling sea, what else to do but
stand aside and watch the fading dread?
Who among us did not believe that some
resurrection song would spring
from his scarred soul and fly
from the ash of a black toe
with him prancing around, wild,

guitar swinging like an uzi at the ready,
ready to make an arch of red in the black night,
like Anancy the come-again artist:
lick im kill im, im bounce right back..?

Tuff Gong cyaan dead!

Who dead? Bob dead? How dead? Long dead.

TURN MY EYES AWAY FROM WORTHLESS THINGS

She was not, so the story goes, the same
    after the rape; her body withered
from her lover's touch. Soon her eyes shifted
    from his gaze. She called their love
a worthless thing – vanity, really,
    as her soul found life in deepest prayer;
everything else became a worthless thing.
    She dumped him in the prayer circle,
declaring before God and the elect,
    the futility of their vain tears,
trying to patch the tatters of an old love –
    a worthless thing before the light of faith;
a piece of scrap wood fit for the flame,
    the licking flame of praise.
So she danced before the Lord,
    sweating out the madness of old memories,
the hurt of her assailant's jabbing.
    She cursed the demon,
her nightly guest, the sweat-slick
    visage of the broken-toothed one
panting out his venom until the silence
    of his spent breathing filled the night.
Then like the rush of water into barren places,
    her voice surged, a wail bearing everything
youthful and giddy in her soul, everything
    of the light and cartwheel of unstoppable laughter,
leaving her cold with the wisdom of years,
    sprinkled with specks of time's dust.
Everything now is worthless, she says,
    everything but the word in season,
the devotion of the self to prayer and fasting.
    Here among the ruins of old love,
she walks on hot granite stones without feeling

the heat or the sharp adze nudging her
callous soles. Her journey is one of naming:
   naming worthless things rightly
is a gift of holiness, a holy gift of God.

SOME TENTATIVE DEFINITIONS V

"Feels so ... right could it last another night"
Ziggy Marley

Watch it when the rapid riddim
bubble like a poco tambourine
over the sound system trembling.
Watch how de dawta dem squat
with dainty decorum of Victorian queens
without the propping of hoops and bones
about to make water in an open field,
and the shape they make
with legs like that
is the frame of a house,
a doll's house with no walls.

Like the way the wave dem come
and go, or two loose windows,
flapping tongues in the wind,
the girl dem causing ripples
on the dance floor. Pure style!
See the coy tilt of the head to the side,
hand resting there on the knees
to keep it all together,
all that water in the waistline;
I can't imagine who call it a butterfly –
what I see is too wet for that,
too water for that, to earth for that.

This vision is a stumbling block,
you know, and if you reading this
you must pray for mercy rain afterwards,
for there is nothing straight and narrow
about the sweet symmetry of this vision.
Me, I am leaning too far forward,
I fall over into the water. It is warm.

IN SEARCH OF FLOWERS

We search for flowers to turn our
fading path once more into
avenues of startling colour; we search
to find another sheath of songs
to embrace, decipher, to learn the new
path taken, path given, way forward,
way to be a poet in this world
of stones falling on roofs, no hands
no chalky hands to betray who threw.

How to exorcise the ghosts who dance
over the white surf of Edgewater
and batter the faithful with stones
falling, falling from the sky?

Who can pray against such magic
without song in the heart,
without the defiant wail of a duppy conqueror,
trailing, trailing like light
from the depths of a prophet's belly?

Where to go without the rhygin reggae dread
prancing in his trance of revelation
in Central Park as if it is
the pimento barbecue of a Nine Mile
farmer's shack; the way the drum
draws a mist over the phallic scrapers,
the stench of a city turning in on itself?

There are no resurrection lilies
in my path, no faith to sustain me;
I have eaten dust for days, and my eyes
are caked with neglected tears.

I feel gummy like a prophet with no story
to tell, no wilderness from whence to return.

Before me are jaundiced leaves
and the worms are eating, eating on their edges.

Where are the songs of the risen?

THE INTANGIBLES OF FAITH

Every act of faith is a carefully drafted contract:
　　a deal with the eternal.
Feed me with words and I will speak for you.
　　The perks, the intangibles
like the smiling accolades of those who hear these words,
　　the awe of the heathen at my wit,
these intangibles do not, must not figure in the deal;
　　they simply clutter transactions.
But each act of faith is a drafted contract.
　　Heal me, and I will walk
the deadly path of ghetto streets offering salvation
　　to the gunman and the thief.
I cleanse my head of the brawta I am sure will come
　　with the deals I make with the almighty.
I wear a poker face while I offer up my blessings,
　　and when the gifts arrive from you,
I accept in hoots of triumph of rejoicing,
　　before I crawl to the quiet of my safe
and count the intangibles, uncountable blessings of faith.

SOME TENTATIVE DEFINITIONS VI
"...let me tell you what I know."
Bob Marley

Police Officer's Club
on Hope Road,
on a wet night,
the teenagers
are turning adult
to the sticky sounds
of Mellow Canary.

I am standing on the edge
smelling too high
of Brut, my silk shirt
already wet with the steam,
hoping she will come
through the croton hedge
like she said she would.

She smiles, calling me
over to the pitch black
of "Bend Down Low,"
and this upright girl
draws me down
so she can tell me
something wet
she knows,
so low,
didn't know
she could ride
so low.

NO MORE THAN YOU CAN BEAR

1

To embrace the gutter is a way to rationalize
 the pain of our suffering. I do this
all the time having savoured and believed
 the assurances of the apostle: No
more than you can bear, no more than...

 Catherine's mind insists it is well
despite the sudden love of tattered cloth
 and garish red bandannas, despite
the crippling of olfactory impulses – she does not
 smell the stale sweat of her many journeys
on sleepless nights, through the sprawling city
 from Half Way Tree to Cross Roads. No
more than she can bear, no more than...

 Michelle sings piercing gospel tunes
on the bus home each night, to silence the mutterings
 of her other voices, clamouring for space
in the sweltering of her crowded brain, telling her
 to climb the hill to his fenced-in home
and announce the will of the Lord to all and sundry,
 prophesying death by disease on his wife;
so she preaches of the lessons learned
 from the squalor of her life. No
more than she can bear, no more than...

 Daily watching the mass of unruly hair
grow denser, more from neglect than as a way,
 a way of defying the middle-class values
of his uptown church, Pedro calls down Babylon,
 and meets with the Twelve Tribes to penetrate
truth, until arrested for carrying weed,

he languishes in the Half Way Tree jail,
writing epistles to the congregation
   who have been praying for the bars to bend,
for Pedro to stroll into their meeting place
   with a testimony of salvation on his lips,
declaring the goodness of the Lord, his promises
   to guide them on this path of squalid pains. No
more than we can bear, no more than...

2

   I wither in the face of pain,
and fall on more carnal comforts to help
   me forget, ignore, be numb to hurt.
I make mute the insistence of my suffering,
   and walk a path of agnostic clarity
while the walls crumble about my head.
   Yet I detest the slime of the gutter
and know of little of worth in the stench;
   I humble myself and plead like a coward
for a way out of the mire. This is my confession
   before heaven and mud. I define the limits
to what I can bear, to what I can possibly bear.

SOME TENTATIVE DEFINITIONS VII

"...I get to understand yuh been livin' in sin"
Bob Marley, "Bend Down Low"

My fifteen year old
ratchet body
welds itself
to her softer front
and I smell Charlie
mingling with the
chemicals in her hair,
and the rest is a song.

Gyrations of heat,
feet not moving
waistlines going,
trying to find
the groove of sweetest
friction, rolling, rolling,
holding on for dear life
like a buoy on a rocking
sea, like a boat
taken out too far from shore.

In my ears her voice
singing: *Row, fisherman, row*

BREAKING THE FAST

1

The sweet bun with pellets of slick raisins
is gummy; the sweating cheese sticks
to the gnaw of my neglected stomach;
I have waited too long for this repast,
fasting in search of the salt of prophecy,
there in Chapel Gardens, in the dry pond.
I sat among stone and bramble waiting for truth
to penetrate the dense, maddening green light;
muttering tongues with blind dispersal of logic,
trying to create my faith from nothing
but a promise of blood from stone.
There was much silence even when the clouds cleared
and light filled the cave of my lamentation.
Now I break my fast with no testimony
of love discovered, truth unearthed,
no impossible word of wisdom, of knowledge
formed in the swelter of my supplications.
I wash down the paste with over-sweet
sky-juice, tart with lime pips.
I swallow quickly, in my haste
freezing my brain. There is no sound for a second –
like the promise of a trance before truth –
then with the thaw comes a nagging ache
that stays with me.

2

Snowy chats with his languid, mournful cadence,
a fatigued eulogy, his forehead grottoed
with old scars, and rivered with older veins;
his mouth clapping, clapping his theories,
alchemized on his sunhot
journey up the hill, carrying his career

in an ancient cart with rough rubber
on wooden spokes for wheels, softer
tubing over his salvaged steering wheel.
He leads a halo of bees everywhere he goes;
such passive bees that respond lovingly to his
every nudge and wave. He is silenced by the tin –
like sound of the transistor chattering out
Trench Town Rock, a refrain to his monologue.

I will be sick from this too quickly devoured
meal, from the yellow sad eyes
of Snowy, from the voice
of another fledgling prophet shouting on
the Stony Hill where they found all the rocks
they needed to spill his brains onto asphalt:
Me cyaan believe it, me seh, me cyaan believe it!
Sounds reverberate like if the fingers of Lee Scratch
done tweak the right buttons, letting the reverb
ride on like a loose kite, until there's an empty space,
a vacuum so hollow it reminds us of tears.

In this quiet, this lapse, there is always
that sweet anticipation of a kicking rhythm section,
hooping keyboard bubbling, a licking guitar scratch –
in this desert there is hope that the dead will rise,
will rise from the dub ruins and patch a new quilt
of sound for the feet to prance on.
It will all return familiar: a fire cooking cornmeal
porridge, old friends, old memories, prayers.
As the evening lags, all remains stark;
the version is eternal, the vacuum deepens,
too dread, too dread, too dub;
nothing explodes, nothing comes back,
nothing wheels and comes again, nothing
but the grunt and scratch of the needle
nudging the last groove, again, and again.
I drift home with sour in my belly.

SHOOK FOIL

1

The whole earth is filled with the love of God.
    In the backwoods, the green light
is startled by blossoming white petals,
    soft pathways for the praying bird
dipping into the nectar, darting in starts
    among the tangle of bush and trees.
My giddy walk through this speckled grotto
    is drunk with the slow mugginess
of a reggae bass line, finding its melody
    in the mellow of the soft earth's breath.
I find the narrow stream like a dog sniffing,
    and dip my sweaty feet in the cool.
While sitting in this womb of space
    the salad romantic in me constructs
a poem. This is all I can muster
    before the clatter of school-children
searching for the crooks of guava branches
    startles all with their expletives and howls;
the trailing snot-faced child wailing perpetual –
    with ritual pauses for breath and pity.
In their wake I find the silver innards of discarded
    cigarette boxes, the anemic pale of tossed
condoms, the smashed brown sparkle of Red Stripe
    bottles, a melange of bones and rotting fruit,
there in the sudden white light of noon.

2

How quickly the grandeur fades into a poem,
how easily everything of reverie starts to crumble.
　　I walk from the stream. Within seconds
sweat soaks my neck and back, stones clog my shoes,
　　flies prick my flaming face and ears;
bramble draws thin lines of blood on my arms.
　　There is a surfeit of love hidden here;
at least this is the way faith asserts itself.
　　I emerge from the valley of contradictions,
my heart beating with the effort, and stand looking
　　over the banking, far into Kingston Harbour
and the blue into grey of the Caribbean Sea.
　　I dream up a conceit for this journey
and with remarkable snugness it fits;
　　this reggae sound: the bluesy mellow
of a stroll on soft, fecund earth, battling the crack
　　of the cross stick; the scratch of guitar,
the electronic manipulation of digital sound,
　　and the plaintive wail of the grating voice.
With my eyes closed, I am drunk with the mellow,
　　swimming, swimming among the green of better days;
and I rise from the pool of sound, slippery with
　　the warm cling of music on my skin,
and enter the drier staleness of the road
　　that leads to the waiting city of fluorescent lights.

SOME TENTATIVE DEFINITIONS VIII

"We gonna rock it baby…"
Bob Marley, "Baby, We've Gotta Date"

In the outdoor chill,
we sip soft drinks.
In this shy silence,
I glance at her face
glowing with sweat,
and her eyes are laughing
with moisture.

Our bodies are startled
by the taboo
of this waltz,
not believing
it has happened
and may happen again
tonight, tonight.

We wait for the cycle
of the disco-jockey
to return to the sticky
mellow of rockers,
silently savouring
the new-found,
the feel of our bodies,
the taste of honey.

When we slide
into the darkest corner
on the tight drum roll,
it is as if we become
water again,
and we embrace like
old pros, no haste,
assured of the sweetness
to come on us like waves.

WHEN THE BRIDEGROOM'S GONE

How can the guests of the bridegroom
fast while he is with them (Mark 2:18)

1

The sisters find new liberty after the cross,
after the darkness on the hill and the slow
procession down to the cave overlooking
the placid sea; after the mourning in austere black,
they eschew the ritual of lamentation for a year,
cycle of dust and ashes, of hot black cotton in Kingston's heat,
and turn to the bright light of calico white
laced with trimmings of gold and silver,
sparkling robes of regal queens, only so far
from the garish announcements of the informal
commercial enigmas who ply the skies
between Miami, Port-au-Prince, Panama City,
San Juan, and Kingston's dry docks,
loudly guarding their purchases with flamboyance.
These queens of the reggae clan prefer silence,
mute royalty, secure in the new light
of ascension. Their jewels have multiplied
where once they carried on their backs
the rugged burlap of poverty, and scrubbed down
plainness of faces unmarked by dyes and inks;
now they have recovered the liberty of female
indulgence: shadow, liner, bright lip-stick
and crowns of such power, they recall Ashanti
mothers, stately walking through the awed city,
their wealth like banners on their skin,
thousand dollar bills sticking to their sweating skins;
they recall a new way of seeing death,
after the nine nights, after the years of
frugal piety, they are finding a way to celebrate
in startling colour and perfumed grace.

But the time will come when the bridegroom
will be taken from them, and on that day they will fast.
(Mark 2:20)

2

While the bridegroom was here, partying was limited
to the whores in the alleyways, the gawking beauty queens.
But now the bridegroom's gone, after the obligatory
lamentation, someone shouted, *It's a soul shakedown party,*
and I can hear the decomposing dread scribing another caustic
pimper's paradise for the three queens,
finding their own, finding their own, like a furlough
after the starvation and blood of the mission field.
I saw them standing beneath a poui tree
on a carpet of yellow leaves, in that soft
of pre-twilight, that tender light filtered
by the green of the hills and hanging trees.
They were listening to the fledgling voice
of the heir apparent and their tears
spoiled the mascara, as they heard the wail
of the bridegroom in the air. They gazed at each other
and smiled through the weeping, maybe for the joy
of knowing that the heir apparent would see their
indulgence and bless it, maybe because they saw
a new path of sound, a new prophet to follow,
this time not as side-kicks, hangers-on, servants
to the king of sound, but as dowager queens,
with hearts full of wisdom and guile, with a way
to make the path better for them. It is this, perhaps,
that made them smile, as they stirred the pouis' blossoms
and floated like magi to the sound of the prince being born;
right, tight reggae mixing up the air
giving light of morning, light of evening, light.

THE PINK MANSION

1

I stand on the edge of the pink mansion
looking for a face in the windows,
a fair skinned face framed by black ropes.
In this falling evening, the light is perfect.
Kingston traffic stirs up the heat and dust,
uniformed children loiter, their faces
stained with dirt and tears, sweat and fruit juice,
kicking stones, boxes, balls, anything to prolong
the slow march homeward; they glut the street
with their colour and their laughter:
this is the beauty of a city at twilight.
The orange I buy from the woman on the corner
is leather-tough with dryness and the juice
too sweet, too warm. Still,
I pull at the flesh and try to suckle quenching
for the barrenness that is before me.
There is no face in the window;
nothing new; yellow sky reflected is all.
Dirt green trees, their leaves shedding;
I hear traffic and blackbirds quarreling.
It is now a museum for the dead.
The ghosts do not linger here.
The heat gathers about me.
The wind stops. Vacuum.

2

On the road to Papine, Shabba causes havoc
on the sound system. I sit between two robust women
who stare into the black road of potholes slipping under us,
wiping sweat from their sturdy faces. Shabba does not make
a mark on anything, on anyone. In Papine the darkness
has arrived. In my soul there is saltiness.

PRAYER FOR MY SON
for Keli

1

When the moist sores sucked strength from your
   frail limbs, I cried out.
Healing came in gradual waves and then you smiled.
   Still, I lie with my silence,
no testimony on my lips, no rejoicing,
   no credit given. I lie.
And there are the days
   of waiting for the wrath to fall,
my punishment for ingratitude,
   collecting miracles like a blooming tree
collects birds, but hides the blossoms
   in skirts of modest green.
Trees have shriveled for less.
   It is written.
This is the quicksand of Babylon,
   dwelling in this place of stagnant logic.
I find even the magic of poems to be forced.
   I live and eat with a people
of calculating guile, who can't see the light
   of a jeweled night for the orange
glow of fluorescent bulbs. When I testify
   in their midst, they fidget
at the gaucheness of my passion, then adroitly
   make humor and little of my faith.

2

These days I barely hear my supplicant moan
    under cover of my dreams.
When morning comes, I quickly forget,
    for how can I expect the magic
of healing when my tongue will not
    speak it, proclaim it, herald it?
I wait for the fire to burn the chafe
    as I watch my child's limbs heal.
It is all I can muster in this barren
    place. My last cry will be
a plea for the unfurling of my tongue
    to draw new paths
in this land of the mute and doubting.
    My last prayer spoken,
I wait for the bright miracle to flame
    in the twilight of peace,
between night and morning, when dew
    is lavender scented and cool,
when the sky is russet soft
    with bated hope.

SOME TENTATIVE DEFINITIONS IX

"Aaaiee! Dis rebel music!"
Marley, "Three O'Clock, Road Block"

this reggae music undulates
like a sheet caught up
by wind

woman
stands silhouetted
by the white of the sheet

the movement of wind
in softer waves
sounds

like dub
crawling across
the belly of the city

poem-making folk like me
seek metaphors
to draw

soundcharts
of the pattern of this
water music, flowing, flowing

but words can only imitate,
and everything barely
catches

the way
reggae sounds on sunday,
lifting the body to softer places

MEETING

In New York, a fancy hotel
where at night tuxedos and gowns
flitter through the lobbies looking for
glamour, bright lights, and a way out,
I enter an elevator and I am overwhelmed by
ites, green and gold tams, black leather
cowboy boots: buffalo soldiers who have found
a subtle marrying of Yard with show-biz affluence.
Lingering sensi tickles my nose.
Nobody speaks: screw faces stare into nothingness,
while the round bass man with inscrutable shades
nods to the clank of the elevator pulleys.
It is the vacuum of silence before
the squeeze of the trigger. I can tell
those eyes have nodded to home-spun executions;
hands washed clean of old blood, but the rankness
of surviving in the squalor still thickens the air.
They stand there poised, priests, before
another revival meeting with the children
falling to the sweet drip-drip of
"Natural Mystic" coming from so far, so far.
That tight, light, lick of the guitar strings
dragged with plastic, fingers touching frets
so light; the sound is sharp edged – *chekeh, chekeh, chekeh* –
until hypnotised the bodies
undulate, one swollen mass
of souls, to that thing coming,
coming through the electric air.
It's like that old grainy photograph,
with world-weary eyes, stern
as if impatient with the cameraman:
Tek de damn ting, man, we got souls to save!
I mutter "irie", announcing my kindred
links to these righteous, altogether

dreads, and all he offers is a nod,
while the drummer slaps a tattoo on his
leather-sheathed thigh.
And as suddenly as the journey began,
I am sucked into a wave,
as if the lobby is a vacuum pulling us.
Leather, cotton, wool, and regal sensi
caress me as they stride by staring ahead.
I am left winded in their wake.Stepping out
into the cold, the wet night swallows them.
I return to the quiet of my hotel room,
slip *Kaya* into the guts of my box.
And I dialogue long and intense
with the mythic declension of the priestly dread,
with his muscular ironies, many journeys,
the classic poesy of a voice, so direct,
so tight, so right, so damned right.

PENTECOST

1

This purple Lenten season,
  we break bread
in the sterile white light of Spring.
  Forgetting old songs,
we sing routine Methodist hymns,
  and in the lightness of after-church
release, the children sprint and squeal,
  whipping up the sweet
irritation of new-mown grass.
  There is no blood
in all of this. No shed blood.
  I leave this place of tidy faith,
and walk through the dusty avenues,
  littered with slow-eyed folk,
nodding in the midday blaze,
  old ones, too frail for the sanctuary,
too cantankerous for the nursing home.

2

  I speak to a trembling woman
on her sun porch, counting days
  before her final journey.
She speaks of the blood ritual
  of slaughtering hogs
down there in Bishopville
  where her daddy share-cropped
for a family as old as the cotton
  that spots the piedmont green like leprosy.
She recalls the metallic smell of new blood,
  a smell that never goes away,

51

always stuck up there in the nose,
   stirring up at each encounter
with violently shed blood.
   The things she has seen:
washing some cousin's life blood
   from the old floorboards
after they carried him miles to die
   before a doctor, with a bullet
in his chest, a knife in his neck.
   She has swabbed pools of blood
off the tiles of the old dispensary,
   and carries the bloody memories
of a lover returned from the blood sports
   of Europe. The blood never stops
in these south lands, it never stops.
   She recalls these memories
like a tenderness in the midday heat.
   Easter is a blood season,
she says, *and to rise into rejoicing*
   from the heaviness of spent blood
is an act of supreme faith; but some mornings
   it is hard as hell to muster the faith
to rise from the swamp of bleeding.
   When I return to the church yard,
the emptiness leaves me lonely;
   I watch the purple cloth of Lent
flutter in the wind; neat as a sermon without blood.

SOME TENTATIVE DEFINITIONS X

"... she had brown sugar all over her boogu-woogu..."
Bob Marley, "Kinky Reggae"

Water pumpy is the
juice squeezed out with
the pressure of rub-a-dub.

This pot is boiling
and all a body knows to do
is stir up the something.

What is it, this thing,
so sweet, so sticky
flowing on my belly like guava jelly?

This is sea water reggae,
wet and salty like sweat,
gleaming on a body in the moon glow.

And after the tart of the sea,
it is like pulpy sweet sop juice
white and potent like spilt seed.

OAKLAND AVENUE

Oakland Avenue reads like a scripture,
a chronicle of the past, the changing dispensations.
 Here the dead speak beyond the grave
through the warped insecurities of the living,
 trying to sustain some orderliness in heaven and hell.
Their resting places, separate houses, divided
 by Sumtonian lines of decency.
The Jewish bones feed from below the tangle
 of jasmine vines, the flowers of lamentation;
the Catholics wait for the trump to sound
 that they may rise and walk the ladder to glory,
shattering the lovingly wrought tombstones in the green;
 the white Baptists rest in Abraham's bosom,
where the lines are clearly drawn – ne'er the twain shall meet;
 and in the unruly corner under the dark of live oaks
rest the Black Baptists, Black Catholics, Black Jews and all.
 For the optimistic, this is a vision of the splendour
of eternity: the accommodation of the dead to neighbours;
 separately equal in the waiting time – there is order here.
But I, walking this avenue late at night,
 smelling the freshness of healthy vegetation,
have imagined the sound of the crazy trumpet,
 imagined the sky flaming with blood red,
the cracking of the old concrete slabs, the handclaps
 of trees stirred by a hot dry wind.
I try to imagine the dead waiting
 in separate lines, despite the pallid sameness
of the worm-cleansed bones, the same dank stench
 of the risen dead. Will the eyes
still be averted, not making four? Will there be songs
 for all to sing? Is not the new robe of resurrection
a garment so complete that all we have thought we are
 will be but a reflection, a pale imitation?
I reflect, here in this place

of multiple fences. Even in death, even in death
our imaginations remain hemmed by a lie.
   Hasten your coming, Saviour, that the question
may be answered clear as new day,
   for our eyes can see little beyond the temporal
and what a miserable condition it is, what a miserable thing.

SOME TENTATIVE DEFINITIONS XI

"Every time I hear the sound of the whip..."
Bob Marley, "Catch A Fire"

For every chekeh of the guitar,
a whip cracks.
How can you hear the sound
and not weep?

Follow the pattern with me,
always on the off.
We are forever searching for spaces
to fill with us.

If you walk straight down on the one,
you will stumble,
cause the reggae walk is a bop
to the off-beat.

We are always finding spaces
in the old scores
to build our homes, temples and dreams,
and we call it back-o-wall.

For every *wooku* of the Hammond B
a body hums.
How can you smell the sound
and still sleep?

SHADOW PLAY
for Akua

Morning birds play shadow games
on my pink light-filtering louvres,
   swoops of grays against the light.
Akua sips the air delicately,
   her eyes fluttering to the moving shadow
of the falling birds, her fists curl,
   punch harmlessly into the air,
while whistles, caws, peeps and squeals
   of birds and insects lull the morning.
My devotions are easier here,
   meditations on the preciousness of life;
I want to swallow, embrace,
   become one with every peace
that suggests itself in the pink and white
   of this morning's communion.
I can believe in miracles in this place.
   My daughter breathes a sigh,
groans, and when I turn from
   the shadow play, her eyes are glittering,
wide open and reading music
   floating in ribbons across the silence.
In her eyes are centuries of seeing,
   as if she has seen all this before,
lived it all before, and sung of it before.
   Before she cries out, I gather her up,
still surprised at the lightness, the bird-like
   vulnerability of her warm, soft body.
She breathes, and breathes and breathes
   like a mantra for new mornings.

SOME TENTATIVE DEFINITIONS XII
"Oh children, children..."

You can tell it's prophecy
by the pronouns used
to carry the revelation.

When the Rastaman,
poet man composer
say, "my children"
to a nation of tears,
say we dis, we dat,
say we dis, we dat,
you know it's prophecy.
Talk yuh talk now,
Prophet man,
Talk yuh talk now,
Prophet man.
      Roots!

GUILTINESS, REST ON YOUR CONSCIENCE

1

For the easing of a guilty mind
the harp played its melody,
the music sweetly cleansing.
The leader, growing fat with power,
caressed the offered nipple,
chocolate-dark and erect
of this new mistress, broadcasting
his idleness in each orgasm
away from the queen, his wife,
who is guarded from assassins
in the official home on the hill.
This syrupy reggae, like an
excursion into the guts of the city,
pulses for him and her, lovers,
making unruly love in the valley heat.
He slums like his life depends on it,
like it is his only way to touch
the masses with his rod of correction,
like those aimless forays
he made into West Indian clubs in London
where his light skin was eclipsed by his
desperate hunger for yard pumpum,
rum, and a way to talk without guarding
against the rule of thumb and tongue
scrutinizing each dragged vowel, each dropped consonant.
And the memory is as familiar
as this red sound in his head
mounting him, whipping him, riding him
to sweat out the blackness beneath
the translucence of his skin.

2

The minstrel
plays his tunes with a grin,
always a grin of his own making,
waiting to go mute with defiance,
opening the chasm between
silver-spooned leader
and the smell of ghetto blood:
Me nuh ave no fren inna high society,
sings the prophet, while the leader
caresses the guava jelly
gathering in pools at the bottom
of the damsel's soul, the
source, the source, the source
of all new arrivals.
There is no marriage between
the reggae man and the leader
but the legend lingers like
a flaming flag of betrayal.
It is morning when the music stops.
Morning is soft and the leader
wends his way to the fortress,
to touch the cheek of his
African wife, sipping the rarefied
air of his election money mansion.
There is the smell of reggae
in the air, drifting up like
the stench of a dog roasting
on burning tire, dark, slow,
but distinct as the smell of death.

BEFORE THE POEM

1

Some things must be left to the logic of the divine;
    if a word declares a path, it is not
our affair to swing machetes, making our own way;
    it is for us only to watch to see the road
appear, made clear for us. And then, with home, walk.
    I have stood upon the mountains
gathered like sentinels around Kingston, such
    purple-green clean in the early evening,
caressed by the swift descent of fog
    while birds dip and soar, towards the grey
of coming night. I have stood on these mountains
    and felt the peculiar safety of a path already made,
of a journey already plotted, tested and taken,
    a time removed from the dry heat of the valley. Now, hands raised,
my head like a livid antennae, I feel
    for the coming word, a way of being in these times.

2

    I tell this now only as a way of recording
a place distinct as the end of prayer: that place
    of hope, before the stark reality
of a still sick child waiting for prayer to take.
    It is a sacred place where poem
is nothing but the dance of new light on grass,
    of music tonguing the quiet of Sunday afternoons:
(this is the hint of a poem about to sprout, long before
    the words are gathered and rendered; there is
a place of calm, an essence that is the fore-poem,
    again, and again, and again, unspoken, but shaped).
I cannot make words here, my limbs move
    building pillars of stone for each revelation.

I do not claim to know the logic of this testament,
   the ubiquitous wisdom of a miracle path,
so I stand dwarfed by a grander design, and wait for
   light in this limbo, wait for illumination.

SOME TENTATIVE DEFINITIONS XIII

"Blow them the full watts tonight"
Bob Marley, "Bold Card"

When the sound kicks in gear,
everything jumping,
the dance hall rocking,
that high hat shimmering,
the bass drum thumping,
and Mr.Bassy unfurls a cord
of spiraling sounds
causing the bodies to spin
like tops unleashed,
what else to do but dance.

And when the brilliant strike
of the guitar licks
like sparkle and tinsel
and the knife blade's edge –
impious, peevish, obstinate,
yet whimsical, and seductive –
straighten the back,
cause the heart to look
to see where it is coming from
this sound, this sound
what else to do but dance.

There is a casket of light at the edge of the garden
that glimmers with the possibility of better times.
From far, it shimmers bright, like the familiar sound of the guitar
chekeh chekeh chekeh chekeh chekeh chekeh

NEW SOUNDS

1

He brought the slip of black vinyl,
and let spin the light on black.
Reggae enigmatic engulfed the house,
and in his blue mist of shelter
he tapped his feet to the new sound:
the jazz subtle in the horn section,
calling up the spirit of Don Drummond,
calling up the side-riding of old jazz folk,
calling up Africa in the dread's journey,
the confirmed journey of the man poet
travelling from first to second to third,
nondescript Trench Town streets, still home
for this pop icon, rude bwoy, skanking dread.
And this is how Thelonious Monk was usurped
from the all wooden, hand-crafted gramophone
cabinet, how the Duke got schooled by a thug,
how a newer path of earth birthing life
suggested itself in our home -- this clean tight reggae,
the I-Threes melodious in their response to his call.

2

On nights when rum poured golden and sweet
and laughter shook the louvres,
I would be called out in my raggamuffin threads
to skank a magic number to Bob's
rocking reggae sound. And dance,
I would dance, owning this sound, owning
this rasta revolution, my body contorting,
mimicking old moves until the spirit of this pulse
would take root; I would do things I never
thought I could, never dreamt I could,

my face a permanent scowl, my feet cool
on the solid tiles, dancing, dancing.
The applause would shimmer,
and beaming, returned from the sea voyage,
my eyes filled with the souls I have met on the way,
I would withdraw to my cubicle room,
nodding to the sibling cheers,
still sweating, still floating,
still amazed at this new way of walking.
The record would kick into gear again,
and the voices would rise in deep discourse,
proclaiming this rhygin man the total socialist dream —
a voice of the people, from the people;
and regretting that they can't package the thing,
can't sell the thing, can only watch in awe, and dance.

BLACK HEART

1

Of the three, one blackheart man lives,
the one whose finger prophesied death
for the Chinese producer, bloodsucker,
pointed to his death, to a heart attack
crashing him down sudden like that,
right there in his office, the crime scene
where hundreds of dreams have been stolen
with a hastily secured signature,
where many voices have been captured
in the cage of black vinyl for a few pounds.
And one normal afternoon, patties consumed,
soft drink gulped quickly, shirt back wet,
after a spate of belching, one vomiting fit,
the man drop dead like that,
lying there like a poem among the carpet
of forty-fives grinning in the fluorescent light.

2

Of the three, one blackheart man lives,
the others are buried beneath the grass,
one the rugged quick tongue of the gangster
dread, stepping razor, crusader of lost causes,
underdog with the wit of a survivor,
his black body boasting bruises
from indiscriminate batons of Babylon's lackeys –
and you can bet he never begged, just cursed
nuff claat, and took the broken jaw
like a trophy – this incarnation
of a Soweto toi toi stumper with no discernible
Boer to make a revolution against,

(for isn't this Paradise where the natives
smile too sweetly to be ruthless?)
just the Shitsem like a windmill.
His eyes would twinkle at the impossible of it
and his mind would construct rastological myths,
the antennae on his head picking up songs
from the waves of the sea at Palisadoes
(and the interviewer nodded with sincere indulgence).
This dread, ambushed by his legacy,
gunned down by an irony so blatant it hurts,
gutted by shot after shot, making him step
searching for solid ground and finding nought
but air, before the head popped. It is finished.

3

Of the three, one blackheart man lives;
the other, the loner, the mystic star-gazer,
the multicoloured coat-wearer, the short explosion,
defied the bullet, but watched
some white man's disease devour his vulnerable
flesh, like treachery, fading, fading
with a whimper against the good night.
The shell could not hold any longer,
crumbled, letting fly his unconquerable soul,
which travelled into mystery and faith;
gone with all the promise,
perhaps because he trusted too much,
perhaps because he embraced too often...

4

Of the three, one blackheart man lives,
the one who will not fly on the iron bird,
not trusting Babylon's contraptions,
sipping, sipping the incense of Jah

and pumping out second-rate dancehall tunes.
A tarnished star, with dubious appeal,
but living through the blackness of a curse,
stoking his own flames of mystery.
He will outlive the poem, he will reorganize
the parts of himself and reinvent his image
before he retires an enigma, a reggae geriatric,
an irrelevant dread with only a satchel
of old songs to his name.Blackheart man,
the true duppy conqueror, showing how rude bwoys
grow grey, showing us the sorrowful mortality
of the skanking old man. The others exploded
in the height of their glory, but he will remind us
that all flesh is dust; even the taut drum skin
of the wailing wailer will shrivel too.
It is how it was written, how it has passed
from generation to generation to generation.

SOME TENTATIVE DEFINITIONS XIV

"one good thing about music..."
Bob Marley, "Trenchtown Rock"

When this slash of a blade,
this blunt object mauling,
this gut grumbling
of subterranean tremors,
causes the body to tremble,
the links of the spine to snap,
when the wash of lyrics
is like an anaesthetic
numbing you to the pain,
what else to do but dance.

There is a memory in the chant
of the lyrics man, conjuring up
that land we have all heard about
and want to see across the sea;
the whip, the gun, the blood
that hurts to hold in the heart,
but this music cools the scorching,
and we are taken by the mystery:
light like a feather, heavy as lead,
so ain't nothing left to do, but dance.

RITA

1

I first saw you cooking in the background
of a jumpy camera shot, while the dread
held forth, constructing his facade of enigma,
dodging the barbs and darts of Babylon with code,
and three times he denied you, called you a sister,
like Isaac did to Rebecca, leaving her there,
hanging like that, open season for Ahimalech
and the boys, that is what you were,
a flower tarnished, just a helping sister,
Martha in the kitchen swollen with child.
And who, watching this, would have known
of the nights he would crawl into your carbolic
womb, to become the man-child again,
searching for a father who rode off on his white steed
and never returned, never sent a message?

2

For years I thought you had lied,
for it was our way to believe the patriarch,
and who would want to declare the coupling
of the downtown dread with the uptown Miss World,
too sweetly ironic, too much of Hollywood
in this sun-drenched, dust-beaten city?
Who would let your black face, weighed by the insult
disturb our reverie? I did not believe the rumours.
So while the nation grumbled and cussed you out,
declared you gold digger and such the like
when he was buried and celebrated in death,
and you published the wedding photos,
the family snapshots of another time;
when you battled like a higgler for rights,

and played every dubious game in the book,
rough-house, slander, ratchet smile and all,
I called it poetic, the justice you received,
for you played the cards right, no bad card drawn
in your hands, as you sat quietly in the back-room
like a nun, bride of Christ and slave to mission.
And when you knew other men
before the tears could dry from our eyes,
and made another child in your fertile womb,
when your garments of silence were replaced
with the garish gold and silver of decadence,
when you entered the studio to play rude girl,
naughty as hell, talking about feeling damned high,
and rolling your backside like a teenager,
I had to smile at the poetic meaning of it all,
for you fasted before this feast,
you played the wife of noble character
eating the bitter fruit of envy
while the dread sought out the light-skinned
beauties, from London, to L.A, King Solomon
multiplying himself among the concubines.

3

These days I have found a lesson of patience
in your clever ways, a picture of fortitude
despite the tears – you are Jamaican woman,
with the pragmatic walk of a higgler,
offering an open bed for his mind-weary nights,
an ear for his whispered fears and trepidations,
and a bag of sand for a body to be beaten,
slapped up, kicked and abused; you took it all,
like a loan to be paid in full at the right time.
I no longer blame you for the rabid battles
raging over the uneasy grave of the rhygin dread;
for now I know how little we know of those

71

salad days in a St. Ann's farmer's one-room shack,
where you made love like a stirring pot,
and watched the stars — for they were the only light.
What potions you must have made to tie, tie
your souls together like this! I simply watch
your poetic flight, black sister, reaping fruit
for the mother left abandoned with a fair-skinned child,
for the slave woman who caressed the head
of some married white master, with hopes
of finding favour when the days were ripe,
all who sucked salt and bitter herbs,
all who scratched dust, scavenged for love,
all who drew bad cards; you have
walked the walk well. The pattern is an old one.
I know it now. It's your time now, daughter,
Ride on, natty dread, ride on, my sister, ride on.

HOW CAN A YOUNG MAN KEEP HIS WAY PURE?

1

The path of the young is strewn
   with stones that have fallen
from an ubiquitous sky. A boy stumbles.
   I travel Kingston's sumptuous lanes,
thick with the green of unruly trees
   and the weekday dreaminess of suburban calm,
eyeing the casual sway of a domestic
   gathering clothes from a nylon line.
She smiles my way only slightly,
   then vanishes into the shadow of a mango tree.
My body is alert to the scent of woman,
   to the slow movement of her body;
and giddy with imaginings,
   I stumble hard from staring into the darkness
trying to draw her out – it is lust I feel,
   fourteen years old and weighed down
by the ambiguities of faith and lust:
   how fervent are my prayers of penitence,
how complete my lustful indulgence.
   I am too young now for middle ground,
though I know I will die forever
   if brought down when my mind is swamped
with the precepts of my libido.
   I seek out purer paths.

2

Few know the canker in my soul.
   I see them see the enigma of a boy,
secret-keeper, a laugh like a wheeze,
   and the mad doggedness to slave
under a stunted breadfruit tree,

73

knocking a cricket ball stuffed in a sock,
with the monotony of a poet in training,
  kock, kock, kock, kock, kock,
each stroke weighted like words before the paper,
  until sweat gathers in a muddy pool
there at the roots of the tree.
  The reggae in my head is a secret too,
I keep it secure along with my lies.
  I do not know love, I do not know faithful;
I know only lust and the paths it makes.
  My prayers wrestle with me
like a poem taking shape in my head.

3

  Sometimes I envy those who follow
the fire and brimstone of the preacher's tongue
  and fall in paroxysms of revelation
there at the altar of light, blissful
  in the consistent path to ecstasy
like the tricks of a couple ten years married,
  making orgasms as routine and dependable
as sleep, food, the idle pleasure of sitcoms.
  I envy them the absence of angst.
My eyes will not stay closed for long,
  I want to see the miracle for myself,
and in my faithlessness I scatter the spirit
  to the other end of the earth.
How can a young man keep his way pure?
  Follow the wind's whisper,
until you reach the end of all walking
  and there, in the moment poised over heaven,
weep, there, weep until
  the water of salts has cleansed and bleached
the flame red of your turbulent soul.
  Then fall with the stones, fall with the stones.

SOME TENTATIVE DEFINITIONS XV

"play I some music..."
Bob Marley, "Roots Rock Reggae"

The *chekeh* of a guitar lick
is the marshall ordering of the troops,
the high cutting edge of sound,
a stick beating you to get up,
to stand to the call, the call,
to grow a callous on your soft soul
so hard it makes the shedding of blood
painless like river-flow to the sea.
This is the militant perpetual
of reggae, roots reggae.
Now you can find the blood of Babylon
in the sky; and hear your voice,
cutting the clutter of other voices
with an irrepressible brilliant licking,
a stiff tongue rubbing a knife edge:
chekeh, chekeh, chekeh, chekeh.
This is the bright outer garment of reggae
catching the noon day light.
Ride on, people, ride on.

ABOUT THE AUTHOR

Kwame Dawes is part of a new generation of Caribbean writers grounded in a tradition which speaks of possibility. He draws upon inspiration as diverse as Derek Walcott, T.S. Eliot, Lorna Goodison, Bob Marley and Peter Tosh.

He was born in Ghana in 1962, moved to Jamaica in 1971 where he remained until 1987. He has also lived in England and Canada. He now lives in America where he is Professor of English at the University of South Carolina. Kwame is an accomplished broadcaster, actor, dramatist and reggae musician.

He has published five collections of poetry, *Progeny of Air*, (Peepal Tree Press, 1994), *Resisting the Anomie* (Goose Lane Editions, 1995), *Prophets*, (Peepal Tree Press, 1995), *Requiem* (Peepal Tree Press, 1996) and *Jacko Jacobus* (Peepal Tree, 1996). *Progeny of Air* won the Forward Poetry Prize for the best first collection of 1994. He is married to Lorna and they have three children, Sena, Kekeli and Akua.